Youtube Marketing

A comprehensive guide to creating, marketing and optimizing video content

Aiden Anderson

Copyright © 2012 Aiden Anderson
All rights reserved.

There's hardly anyone who has never heard of YouTube - or never spent an afternoon watching one cat video after another. YouTube is a great source for fun, entertaining content. But the platform is also becoming more interesting for marketers. The current **State of Inbound report** shows that nearly half (48%) of all marketers plan to include YouTube in their marketing strategy over 12 months (from the survey date).

You may doubt that your audience is also active on YouTube. But are you quite sure?Statistics show that the majority of internet users watch videos online, And YouTube has **more than 1 billion active users**. The platform's offer is so large that it covers content in 76 languages, covering **95% of the world's population.** If you are still unsure, take a look at these statistics:

- **3.25 Billions of hours** of video content is viewed on YouTube every month
- **On mobile devices alone**, YouTube reaches more users at the age of 18-49. Than all the news channels and the cable television.
- **59%** All leaders prefer videos to content in text form

First, it's very likely that your audience uses

YouTube. On the other hand, the platform is also **the second largest search engine**, making it a great way to optimize your search engine and strengthen your overall brand image. On YouTube, marketers can present content in a unique format that is easy to consume and share.

Since the concept of YouTube marketing may seem intimidating at first, we've created a comprehensive guide with lots of helpful information - for YouTube professionals and newcomers alike. We'll walk you through how to set up a YouTube channel, optimize search engine videos, launch an ad campaign on YouTube, and interpret metrics about your videos.

If you currently do not have time to read the guide completely, you can bookmark it for later reading, or just jump to the section that interests you most:

- **Create a YouTube channel**
- **Optimize videos for search engines**
- **Create videos for YouTube**
- **Market a YouTube channel and YouTube videos**

YouTube Marketing (Aiden Anderson)

A comprehensive guide to creating, marketing and optimizing video content

- An introduction to YouTube Analytics
- Conduct a YouTube ad campaign

CONTENTS

1	CREATE A YOUTUBE CHANNEL	1
2	OPTIMIZE VIDEOS FOR SEARCH ENGINES	10
3	CREATE VIDEOS FOR YOUTUBE	18
4	MARKET A YOUTUBE CHANNEL AND YOUTUBE VIDEOS	30
5	AN INTRODUCTION TO YOUTUBE ANALYTICS	35
6	CONDUCT A YOUTUBE AD CAMPAIGN	41
7	CONCLUSION	44

1) CREATE A YOUTUBE CHANNEL

First of all, we would like to point out that having your own YouTube channel does not mean a lot of administrative and planning effort.

Unlike other social media platforms, YouTube only hosts videos. If you only create your YouTube channel to upload a specific video, but you do not intend to continue to maintain your channel, we advise against it. Having your own YouTube channel requires that you take the time to plan, create, edit, market, and analyze your content - all the while. You also need to understand what your goals are with your brand, and then think about how to better achieve them with video content. But when you're ready to make the effort, you'll be rewarded with attractive, sharable content and a growing audience.

Create an account

Your first step is to set up a YouTube channel. And that is not very straightforward. As you know, YouTube belongs to Google. Therefore, when you create a Gmail account, you also have the option to set up a YouTube account or Google + account, and so on. Depending on the nature of your business, it may be more or less advisable to associate your email account with your YouTube business channel. This is especially true if you allow access to your account for your employees or agency partners. We recommend that you create a generic e-mail account that can be easily shared by multiple users.

Call Google.com and click the top right of "**Login**".

Click "**Create Account**" at the bottom of the window.

Enter the following information: your name, the desired e-mail address plus password, your birthday, your gender, your telephone number and current e-mail address as well as your country. Then click Next". Please note that Google only allows users who are at least 13 years old.

Agree to Google's Privacy Policy and Terms of Service and verify your account by entering the code you received by SMS or phone call.

Congratulations, you now have a Google Account.

Set up a company account or brand account on YouTube

Before you can publish content to YouTube after you've created your Google Account, you'll first need to set up a so-called YouTube Brand Account. You need this account to manage editing rights and optimize your overall online presence.

Go to the **YouTube.com** page. If a person icon appears in the upper right corner, you are already logged in. If this is not the case, the "Login" button appears at the same place. Click on it and enter the username and password of your Google Account.

Then click on "**My Channel**" in the account menu in the upper right corner.

Here you can now create a channel directly. But do not click on the "Create Channel" button, but instead on "**Company Name / Other Name**".

Enter the name of your Brand Account and click on "**Create**". Note: You can change the name of your channel later using your account settings.

Next, adjust the settings of your Brand Account. Click on "**Customize channel**".

First select a channel icon and a channel picture. These are the first two items that users see when they visit your YouTube channel. So be sure to choose pictures that your target audience recognizes and matches with your brand.

The channel icon is similar to the Facebook profile photo. The image you select here will also be used for your other Google accounts, such as Gmail or your Google + account. For companies, the company logo offers itself here, for public figures a professional portrait.

To upload a channel icon, click the default red profile picture on the upper left corner of your channel. Now you can select a picture. From

Google recommend a square format to use 800 × 800 pixels or a round image. Note that it may take a few minutes for your uploaded channel icon to appear.

Next, add a channel picture. To do this, click on the blue "Add channel image" button at the top center of your channel. It's a good idea to choose a 2560 × 1440-pixel image suitable for all viewing modes, so you can see it on desktops, tablets, smartphones, and televisions. If you are not sure about the design of your channel picture, you can follow the **templates provided by YouTube**.

Then select the Channel Info tab and add a description, your business email address, links to your corporate website, and social media profiles to your channel. The Channel Description field is designed to introduce your business and explain what type of video content you want to provide on YouTube. Since the channel description is search engine relevant and you can thus influence your search engine ranking, you should definitely include relevant keywords. Below you will find more detailed tips for optimizing your channel description.

In the next step, you can further customize your account. But one important piece of information in advance: YouTube gives you the ability to set up two different views of your channel - one for your subscribers and another for non-subscribers. This means that viewers who have not yet subscribed to your channel are recommended to use content other than their subscribers. A pretty handy feature!

One of the biggest advantages of this feature is that you can create a channel trailer - the video version of your channel description - that will be shown to non-subscribers only. Your trailer should be short (30 to 60 seconds) and meaningful. Its purpose is to attract new subscribers and show users what your channel is about and what content they can expect there. Trailers are generally not interrupted by advertisements so as not to distract viewers from their original purpose.

First, make sure that the "Adjust channel layout" function is activated. To do this, click the gear icon on the top right of your channel next to the Subscribe button.

If you have not already done so, activate the function "Adjust channel layout" and then click on "Save".

Now you can upload your trailer. Click the upload button (up arrow) in the top right corner and select the desired video file. Do not forget to mention keywords in the name and description of your trailer. After you've uploaded the video, select the Summary tab and then For New Visitors. Then click on "Channel Trailer".

Now select the uploaded trailer or specify the URL of the video to be played at this point. Then click on "Save".

Note: If your channel has more than 100 subscribers, was created more than 30 days ago, and you've already added a channel icon and image, you may be eligible to create a custom URL.

Before you start implementing your YouTube marketing strategy, it's a good idea to first determine which of your employees need access to your YouTube account. By giving people access, they can help you manage their YouTube account through their own Google Accounts.

You have three different roles that you can assign to other users of your Google Account.

- **Owner**: Owners have full permissions to manage all of your Google Accounts on all Google services. You can add and remove administrators, edit company information, respond to comments, and more.
- **Administrator**: Administrators have the same permissions as holders, except for delete entry and access management rights. Only owners and administrators have the right to manage your YouTube channel.
- **Communications Administrator:** Communications administrators can respond to comments and take a few more actions. You can not access the video manager and can not upload content or view analytics data.

To add more users to your account, click the

gear icon in the upper-right corner of your channel. Select "Account," and then click "Add or remove administrators."

Click on "**Manage permissions**".

To add new users, click the people icon in the top right corner.

Now enter the Gmail address of the user you want to grant the permission to and assign it a role.

2) OPTIMIZE VIDEOS FOR SEARCH ENGINES

So your YouTube channel is fully up and ready to publish content. Then it is only necessary to make sure that this is also found. As mentioned above, YouTube is the second largest search engine, and while it is undoubtedly critical to provide attractive content, there are certainly other success factors to consider. There are several ways to optimize your videos so that they appear at the top of search results on both YouTube and Google.

The first step on the way to professional YouTube marketing is to edit and optimize your metadata. Metadata basically provides users with additional information about their videos. Examples include: video title, description, tags, categories, thumbnails, and subtitles. What data you specify here is important because videos are indexed based on the metadata and listed in the search results. So it depends on the metadata, whether users actually find your videos. Formulate meta-data always as short and concise as possible. And keep in mind that your content may be removed if you select keywords that are not relevant to your content.

title

Just like with on-page SEO, the wording and description of videos is also crucial for videos. When users scroll through a list of videos, they first read their titles. Therefore, they should necessarily be meaningful and interesting. A title should either arouse interest or convey at first glance that users find a solution to their problem here. Search keywords to get a better idea of which keywords users are using. Put the most important information and keywords at the beginning of titles and use only about 60 characters, so that titles are completely displayed in the search results and not truncated.

description

Note that on YouTube, only the first two to three lines (approximately 100 characters) of the video description appear. To read the entire description, users must first click on "Show More". Therefore, you should always include important links and CTAs at the beginning of the description. The text itself should be formulated so that as many users as possible access your video and interact with your content. Under the description you can insert the transcript. This is useful because videos generally contain many keywords, and so you can improve your ranking. You can also include a default channel description with links to your social media profiles, contributor information, and times. Video titles and descriptions may also contain # hashtags. Just be careful not to overdo it.

Tags

Once you've inserted your keywords in the title and video description, you can use tags to highlight key keywords. Tags are used to link videos with similar videos, thus increasing their reach. Be sure to tag the key keywords first, and use both general keywords and specific long-tail keywords.

category

After you've uploaded a video to YouTube, you can assign it to a category through advanced settings. Video categories are designed to link your content to other, similar YouTube content. You can choose from the following categories: Film & Animation, Cars & Vehicles, Music, Animals, Sports, Travel & Events, Games, People & Blogs, Comedy, Entertainment, News & Politics, Practical Tips & Styling, Education, Science & Technology and social commitment.

Thumbnail

A video thumbnail is the preview image of a video, which is the image users see as they scroll through a list of videos. The image displayed here can have a significant impact on the number of views your video receives. While YouTube will automatically suggest some thumbnail options, we encourage you to create and upload your own. According to **reports from YouTube** 90% of the most successful YouTube videos have a custom thumbnail. So make sure when shooting the video that you have some high-quality and meaningful images for the thumbnail. According to YouTube, it's best to choose a 1280 × 720 pixel image to make sure it's displayed optimally on any screen or display.

Note: You must confirm your YouTube account to upload a custom thumbnail. Just go to **youtube.com/verify** page , get a verification code and enter it.

SRT files (subtitles)

Subtitles are not only helpful to viewers, but also for you. It's another opportunity for you to bring in key keywords, helping you optimize your videos for search engines. To add subtitles to a YouTube video, simply upload a subtitle file, including any timecodes, in one of the supported file formats. You can also upload the full transcript and set it to auto-timing, enter the subtitles or their translation during video playback, or hire an expert to transcribe or translate your video.

If you want to add subtitles to a video, open **Video Manager** and click Video under Video Manager. Find the video in question and open the Edit drop-down menu. Select the "Subtitles" option. Now you can choose how you want to add subtitles.

Cards and Discounts (Notes)

In May 2017, YouTube discontinued the annotation editor. Instead, now cards and the credits are used to interview viewers and to link external websites and other videos. But do not worry! Cards and tabs are as easy to add to a video as annotations. **Cards** are small rectangular format messages that **display** in the top right corner of both desktop and mobile devices. You can add up to five cards to each video. However, be sure to place them so that your viewers have enough time to complete the action you want.

To add a card, open the Video Manager and then the Edit drop-down menu. Select the option "Cards" here.

Click Add Card and select the type of card you want: Video or Playlist card, Channel card, Voting card or Link card.

After you have created the card, you can simply drag it to the desired location in the video. Your changes will be saved automatically.

Abrasive give you the option to extend your video by 5 to 20 seconds and use that extra time to alert your viewers to other YouTube videos or channels and add external links, such as to your website. Relaxation is what motivates users to continue interacting with your content or brand.

Add a credits as follows: Open the Video Manager and then the Edit drop-down menu. Select here the option for cut-off and annotations.

Then select the items you want to add to your credits. You can either import the credits of another video, use a YouTube template, or create items manually. Please note that YouTube's policies require that you refer to at least one other YouTube video or playlist in the credits.

Playlists

If your videos cover a few topics, playlists are for you. Because they allow you to combine different videos on the same topic, including videos from other channels in a playlist. With playlists, you can organize your videos in a clear way and propose a new user at the end of a video. Best of all, playlists are listed separately in the search results. When you create playlists, your content is found faster.

To create a new playlist, go to a video you want to include in this playlist and then click the icon below the video . Select "Create a new playlist". Give the playlist a name and click "Create".

3) CREATE VIDEOS FOR YOUTUBE

Once you have set up your channel, you can already publish first content. In this section, you'll learn what to watch out for when recording videos, how to edit videos, and what types of videos you can post on YouTube. If you are not sure where to start, it may help you to look at a few examples of successful promotional videos and video campaigns . Maybe these will give you some ideas for your next project.

8 different types of videos

Before you start recording video, think about the type of video that will most effectively accomplish your goal. Keep in mind that the different video types are different in importance and effective. The most successful YouTube marketers ranked the types of videos as follows, according to an article in The **Huffington Post:**

A comprehensive guide to creating, marketing and optimizing video content

1. Testimonials from customers

These are short interviews with satisfied customers. They increase the audience's confidence in your company and your product.

2. On-demand product presentations

Demo videos provide a brief introduction to the features and benefits of a product.

3. Informative videos and tutorials

In videos of this type, users are given detailed explanations of how to use a particular product or different components of a product or service. Tutorials are great for answering customer questions or introducing a new feature of a product.

4. Interviews with thought leaders

Interviewing experts or thought leaders can help you build a reputation in your industry.

5. Project evaluations and case studies

Project reviews or case studies show successful campaigns or projects, often based on statistics and results.

6. YouTube Live

YouTube Live serves as the name implies, the live broadcast of content. With live streaming, you can easily share your audience with special moments, as well as giving them the ability to comment on and interact with your content in real time. Live videos will also be recorded and added to your uploaded videos.

7. Videoblogs

Videoblogs are used to share videos that document your everyday life or specific events. These videos are usually published daily or weekly. You can also use this type of video to For example, you can briefly summarize the most important points and tips of a blog post and make this information accessible to your target group in another format.

8. Eventvideos

With this type of video you record a conference or fair etc. from the perspective of the participants. These videos are great for capturing the mood of the participants.

Create a video script

objective

As with all other campaigns and content, it is crucial that you first determine what you want to achieve. For example, do you want to increase brand awareness, increase inbound traffic to your website, gain more subscribers to your channel, or get your content shared more often? Be sure to set a primary goal for your video at the beginning of your production process, so you can focus on the script and your strategy. While you can set different goals for your YouTube channel, such as increasing brand awareness and gaining more subscribers, etc., videos should be limited to one goal.

Create the storyboard and write the text

Once you've decided on a destination, you can start creating your storyboard. A storyboard visualizes the script and serves to plan the individual scenes of a video. Maybe you have even seen one before. Storyboards are similar to comics. They contain rough sketches of the planned scenes, including brief descriptions as well as information about dialogue and camera position and movement. Which details you include in your storyboard is of course up to you. However, we strongly recommend that you include the following:

- A frame for every important scene and every new location
- A rough description of each scene (time of day, weather, mood of the actors etc.)
- The text of each scene
- Information about the camera work and to which filing is to be made

Plan additional multimedia elements

If you plan to include multimedia elements such as charts, a cover image, or similar in your video, plan to do so from the start. Include them in your storyboard to make sure each content element blends seamlessly into each other.

Set the length of the video

As you build your storyboard, set the length of your video as well. On YouTube, videos that are less than two minutes long are the most popular. Limit yourself to the key points you need to mention to achieve the goal set in step 1. For longer videos, you should make sure that you do not lose the interest of the audience. Just experiment with the tempo, story arc and visual elements.

Choosing the right location (s)

Once you've set the goal and length of your video and finished the storyboard, it's time to start thinking about the location. In the film industry, this step is referred to as location scouting and just as with any other step, your choice also has a decisive effect on the success of your video. To choose the right location, you should first pick up your storyboard and make a list of all the places in it. How many locations you need depends on your concept and can vary from one location per video to one location per scene.

When looking for the right locations, friends, colleagues, and family members can be of great help. Note that at some locations (such as businesses and other privately owned buildings), you may film with permission only. Especially with your first productions, we recommend that you do not make life unnecessarily difficult, and therefore limit yourself to locations that can convey to friends and acquaintances.

Make sure you visit the planned locations in advance of the recording and check whether the planned recordings are really possible there. In general, it is beneficial if you have as much space as possible so that you can flexibly adjust the camera position. Also, be aware of loud roads or other noises such as the noise of air conditioners, etc., that could disturb your record. Also check the lighting conditions and do not forget to consider the time of day. Because it can be, for example, that a room is bright enough in the morning, but in the afternoon or evening you need additional electrical lighting.

6 tips for recording professional videos

Recording professional video today no longer requires an expensive camera or budget. The technology of smartphone cameras is now so advanced that their quality is completely sufficient. However, if you are recording a video with your smartphone, be careful to keep it at a minimum. By default, since YouTube displays videos in landscape orientation, you will avoid unfavorable cropping or framing of the video when uploading to YouTube. Regardless of the camera used, these tips will help you create professional and engaging videos:

1. Use a tripod

Finally, you want your viewers to focus on the content of the video, not the shaky camera work. For static shooting, use a tripod or place the camera on a flat surface.

2. Activate the manual mode

If possible, do not use any automatic adjustment , so you can set the focus, exposure, and other settings yourself.

3. Film from different angles and distances

Film each scene from multiple perspectives so you can later select from different clips when editing. For example, in interviews or other recordings where there is only one person in the picture, you can switch from the front view to the 45-degree view. In addition, you can add a little variety to your recordings by increasing or decreasing the distance between the person and the camera or by zooming in or out. By switching between different angles and distances, the video remains interesting and appealing.

4. Film more material than you need to

In retrospect, cutting out scenes is no problem. But you do not always have the opportunity to return to the location for further recordings. So gather enough material by shooting multiple takes of each scene. Also, count to five at the start of the recording and at the end of the scene to make sure you have everything important on tape.

5. Use camera shots

If you have a slider or steadicam available, you can put a little movement into play. It is enough to swivel the camera slightly from left to right, or to zoom in on the object at short notice to make your video more interesting.

6. Use a high quality microphone

If people in your video are talking, be sure to use a high-quality microphone. There are numerous microphones available with which the sound can be recorded separately during video recording. There are even microphones that can be connected to smartphones to improve their audio quality.

Prepare videos

Tools

There is a large choice of editing tools and software. Depending on the operating system, your computer may already have a free editing software such as iMovie or Windows Movie Maker preinstalled. These programs provide basic video editing features. For example, you can use them to crop clips, add titles, and use some limited filtering and color correction features. You can also use professional video editing software such as Final Cut Pro X or Adobe Premiere CC. These are not cheap, but offer many editing functions. Alternatively, **some editing** features are available **on YouTube**. For example, you can merge individual clips into one video there.

Video-Thumbnails

When you upload a video to YouTube, you can select the thumbnail that appears on your channel, in the search results, and in the column to the right. We recommend uploading your own custom thumbnail.

watermark

YouTube gives you the ability to add a custom watermark to your videos. This is a custom button that allows viewers to subscribe to your channel while watching one of your videos.

Open the Creator Studio. Click on "Channel" and then on "Branding". Then follow the instructions to upload your file.

Music and sound effects

The quality of the music and sound effects of a video can determine whether a video is perceived as a professional production or as the work of a layman. Fortunately, a small budget for professional sound effects is enough these days. When selecting the music for a video, you should orientate yourself to the mood in which you want to move the audience. Music is one of the most effective ways of influencing what emotions a video causes its viewers. Often even editors, cameramen and actors orientate themselves on the music. If you present your brand to a new target group, for example, cheerful, peppy music is recommended. Another very important aspect to consider when choosing music is usage rights. Be sure to select only royalty-free tracks. Although royalty-free does not mean that you can use the music for free. However, you only pay a flat fee once for these titles and you do not have to pay any additional royalties or license fees.

YouTube has a whole **library of sound** effects and music that you can use for free in your videos. Alternatively, you can find premium royalty-free music on **Pond5**, **Epidemic Sound** and **PremiumBeat**. There you can choose from countless professionally recorded and produced titles from various genres and with different lengths and tempos. PremiumBeat and Pond5 both offer an extremely comprehensive collection of sound effects to help give your videos more character. Sometimes some subtle sound effects in the background are enough to raise the quality of a video and cast a spell over its audience.

4) MARKET A YOUTUBE CHANNEL AND YOUTUBE VIDEOS

But with the production of videos and their search engine optimization it is not done yet. Because now the marketing of your channel and your content is about to begin. The ideal goal is, of course, a broad base of subscribers and the best possible position of your content in the search results. But especially for newcomers, this is not always easy to achieve. So it's important to promote your YouTube channel and videos on other platforms as well. Conveniently, both YouTube and other platforms offer features that make sharing videos easy. And this is the best way to promote your YouTube content on other channels:

Social Media

Sharing your YouTube videos on social networks

is an easy way to raise awareness and interact with viewers. YouTube makes it very easy for users to share and promote videos on other channels. Just click the Share button below the video you'd like to share. You can then select the platform on which you want to promote the video. YouTube even creates shortened URLs for videos so you can share them even more easily.

You should be strategic in marketing your YouTube channel and videos. So there are more effective ways than just sharing your videos in your timeline or feed. Think about the purpose for which you produced the video. For example, if you've created a tutorial because you've had a lot of questions about using your product, it's a good idea to answer those questions with the link to this tutorial. Videos created in a campaign or global trend should be tagged with relevant # hashtags to maximize their reach.

Blog posts and websites

Advertise your YouTube channel and videos on your website and blog. First, make sure your YouTube channel is better by adding a button to your website and blog that allows visitors to follow your YouTube channel. Then embed relevant videos into your website or blog posts. For example, you could create a YouTube video as companion to a specific blog post or share customer reviews or case studies in video format on your website. It not only promotes your YouTube channel and videos, but also increases your website **traffic**.

To share a video on your website or blog, copy the embed code that appears below the video.

Email

Be careful not to neglect your existing customers due to their efforts to attract new customers and leads. Advertise your videos and YouTube channel using relevant email lists. Encourage your contacts to watch a blog post in which you have embedded a video to increase the reach of the video as well as your website traffic. If you have created a playlist that fits the theme, you can also draw attention to it. E-mail newsletters with helpful information and content are an effective way to promote customer loyalty.

Websites for questions and answers

If your videos provide answers to specific questions, you can share them on popular Q & A sites, such as **Quora, to raise awareness of** your business and content. See what questions are asked there and, if necessary, share videos that help users.

Teamwork

Do you have connections to a company that is well represented on YouTube? If so, then just ask for collaboration, such as creating a video or playlist together. Such cooperation is beneficial for both sides as the reach of each channel is extended to the other party's target group. The possibilities for creative cooperation with other companies are manifold. Just be sure to choose companies whose goals and audiences are similar to your own. In addition, the partnership should be compliant with your marketing strategy.

Interact with viewers

It's important that you interact with your audience. Review comments, answer questions, ask for feedback, and thank your viewers for their support. Since these are tasks that are quickly neglected, we recommend that you periodically take specific time to review and respond to the comments on your videos.

5) AN INTRODUCTION TO YOUTUBE ANALYTICS

After investing so much time and energy into your YouTube channel, content creation, search engine optimization, and marketing, you'll want to know the extent to which these efforts pay off.

Do not be shy if you're not familiar with **YouTube Analytics** at first . So many ratios and charts can be confusing at first glance. The good news is that once you look at it, you'll see that the metrics can basically be interpreted quite simply.

Set a clear goal

First of all, it's important to understand how crucial it is to focus your videos on a specific goal. If you do not set a goal, you will not be able to measure results. Videos should be geared to a specific purpose from start to finish - from shooting to editing to upload, to optimization and publishing.

It is advisable to choose one goal per video. Videos are most often created **to increase brand awareness, get more views or clicks, generate more inbound links, and get more social media shares**. For example, depending on how you incorporate videos into your marketing activities, you can increase the opening rate of an e-mail series or increase the conversion rate of a landing page. YouTube is a great way to increase brand awareness.

As mentioned, YouTube is the second largest search engine. Videos you publish there appear on the one hand in the organic search. On the other hand, you can draw attention to them through paid ads. Videos help you build a personal relationship with your audience by empowering your employees, customers and partners personally. In addition, you can use video to increase the confidence of your target customers in your business by sharing content that will help them. Which type of video you choose depends, among other things, on whether you promote the video through paid ads or opt for organic search optimization. If the latter is the case, customer reviews, product tutorials, or a company history video are recommended.

mportant key figures

Getting started with analyzing the metrics on your YouTube videos can be a bit frustrating. But it is important that you measure your success. On the other hand, it is also frustrating when one of your videos receives much less attention than expected. Use YouTube Analytics to see how your video was found, how long visitors viewed it, and how they interacted with it. So let's take a look at which metrics YouTube Analytics captures and where you can find them.

Go to the **youtube.com/analytics page**. Now you should see an Analytics dashboard with an overview of the performance of your videos over the past 28 days. You can also select a different time period using the drop-down menu in the upper right corner. The summary report provides key performance metrics, engagement metrics, demographics, traffic sources, and information about your most successful content.

You can also apply the following filters to the results: Content, Device Type, Region or Location,

All Uploaded Content, or Only Playlists, Subscriber Status, Playback Type, YouTube Product Traffic, and Translations Used. In addition, you can view the results in various charts or even an interactive map.

The metrics you use to measure the success of a campaign depend on many different factors, but there are a few things you should keep in mind:

Watch time and viewer loyalty

The Watch Time report shows how much time (in minutes) viewers have spent watching content on your channel, both in total and per video. This will allow you to check which videos your viewers actually watch, and which they just click on and then cancel. The **playback time is** an important index as it is one of YouTube's ranking factors. The longer the watch time of a video, the higher the likelihood that it will get a good search engine ranking. YouTube also provides the ability to report on specific metrics, including watch time, views, average watch time, and the average percentage of video playback. You can review these metrics for individual videos, locations, publication dates, and more. The average percentage of video playback shows how much viewers viewed an average video on average (per call). The higher the percentage, the higher the probability that viewers watch the entire video. Include cards and video clip in videos that are high enough to make your calls-to-action more frequent.

Traffic sources

The Views traffic source report shows how viewers found your content. It will give you valuable information about where to promote your YouTube content best. For example, you can use the report to see if viewers found your content on Twitter or through YouTube Search. Under the general menu item "Traffic sources" you will find even more detailed information. Based on this data, you can then optimize your YouTube marketing strategy. Do not forget to improve your metadata as well.

Demographic data

The demographics report provides data on the age and gender of your viewers and helps you to better define your audience. This allows you to additionally filter the age group and gender data according to other criteria such as the location. With this report, you can more accurately match your content to your YouTube audience and see how well they are coming to your **Buyer Personas**.

Interaction reports

These reports tell you which content is most popular with your audience. They contain information about which content is clicked, shared, commented, and recommended. In addition, you will find data on the performance of cards and discounts here. These data are helpful because they tell you what content your audience is interacting with. You can then use this information to optimize the CTAs in your future videos.

6) CONDUCT A YOUTUBE AD CAMPAIGN

In addition to promoting organic traffic, you can also use several paid ad options to promote your YouTube videos. In this section, we'll introduce you to creating YouTube ad campaigns.

Cost of YouTube ads

The cost of YouTube ads depends on the number of views. This means that only actual interactions with the ad will be charged to you. If your ad is skipped, there are no costs. The exact price per click depends on the popularity of your keywords and is about $ 0.06 on average. After you set a daily budget for your campaign, your ad will run until that daily budget is exhausted.

The different types of YouTube ads

Video Discovery Ads

TrueView Video Discovery ads appear on YouTube on the homepage, in search results, and on watch pages in suggested videos. If you click on such an ad, the associated video is called.

In-stream video ads

In-stream video ads are ads embedded in a YouTube video. TrueView in-stream video ads play at the beginning of a video. You can add text or CTA overlays to them, and users usually have the option to skip the video ad after five seconds. For videos that are over 10 minutes long, in-stream video ads can be placed not just at the beginning of the video, but during the video as well.

Create a campaign

You can **create** a **campaign from** any video you have uploaded to your YouTube channel. Open your **Google AdWords account**.

Add the video you want by copying its YouTube URL and pasting it in the box next to Video Ad.

Write a headline and a description that will

appear in the search results and choose a thumbnail.

Determine where users are directed after they click on your ad: on your YouTube channel or website.

Choose a daily budget for your ad and specify how much you want to pay per call.

Indicate in which regions the ad should be displayed. You also have the option to exclude certain areas.

The next step is to define the audience of your ad by selecting the demographic and psychographic data you want. These include age, gender, interests, and more. Link your AdWords account to your YouTube channel and complete the build. This automatically activates the ad.

7) CONCLUSION

With **more than a billion active users**, YouTube is now much more than a platform for fun, entertaining content. YouTube has become an important marketing platform that gives you the opportunity to promote your brand with visual content. And videos can **increase your organic traffic by 157%**.

Be sure to promote your YouTube channel and videos as part of your inbound marketing strategy. Create content that tells an interesting story and provides helpful information to viewers. Advertise this content on all channels, including social media, email, your corporate blog, and your website. Optimize your content with cards, discounts and clear CTAs.

The concept of YouTube marketing may seem a bit overwhelming at first glance. Basically, it's easy to share content on the platform. Your audience is waiting to see and interact with informative and entertaining video content. So follow our tips and find your optimal YouTube marketing strategy!

www.ingramcontent.com/pod-product-compliance
Lightning Source LLC
Chambersburg PA
CBHW051203170526
45158CB00013B/1079